THE GR ESCAPE

Written by Tony Bradman
Illustrated by Steve Stone

Robin's mum was reading the newspaper.

"Grrr, that horrible Sheriff," she muttered. "I wish the nasty man was here so I could tell him off."

"Er … I think he is, Mum!" said Robin.

"How dare you!" snarled the Sheriff. "Take her to the castle, men – and seize the boy!"

"Run, Robin!" yelled Mum.

Robin hid behind a market stall and watched the soldiers dragging Mum off. He felt very alone – and afraid. "I need some help," he thought.

So he ran to his friend Marian's cottage, and told her what had happened.

"We have to save my mum!" Robin said.

"Umm ..." said Marian. "I wonder if there's a way we can get into the castle secretly?"

"Great idea!" said Robin. "And I know how we can find out!"

They soon found a book with a plan of the castle.

"Look, there's a secret door," said Marian.

"Come on," said Robin. "There's not a moment to lose …"

They discovered the secret door and crept through it into the Sheriff's castle. Then they tiptoed down a dark, narrow passage.

"Ugh! I hate spiders," muttered Robin.

At last, they came out into a large room lit by candles.

"Now what?" hissed Marian.

Suddenly they heard someone shouting.

"That sounds like my mum!" said Robin.

Robin gently pushed the door open. Mum was standing in front of the Sheriff.

"You're a very bad man, Sheriff!" she scolded. "People are starving because of your taxes."

"I've had enough of you," growled the Sheriff. "Throw her in a dungeon!"

"You won't get away with this!" yelled Mum, as the soldiers dragged her off.

Robin and Marian followed them down the castle's dark steps and passages.

"In you go!" said a soldier. He pushed Mum into a smelly dungeon.

Robin was angry, but Marian held him back. "Look!" she hissed.

The soldier had left his keys in the lock. Robin and Marian waited until he had gone, and then they let Mum out of the dungeon.

Mum was very surprised.

"Let's get out of here!" said Marian.

They headed down a passage, and another, then round a corner ...

… where they bumped into some more soldiers!

"Oof!" said one of them.

"Whoops!" said Robin.

"Grab them!" said another soldier, but it was too late …

Robin, Marian and Mum ran through the castle searching for another way out. Soon they were being chased by lots of soldiers, and lots of other people too.

"I'm running out of puff!" said Mum.

At last they came out into the castle yard. "A horse and cart. Great!" said Marian. "You two jump in the back – I'll drive!"

Marian drove the cart across the castle yard. The gate was still open, but she knew they didn't have much time.

"You don't have to hold on to me quite so tightly, Mum!" said Robin.

The Sheriff and some of his men were chasing them on horseback now, and they were catching up very fast.

"We'll never outrun them!" cried Marian.

They rushed out of the gate. Robin looked all around. Suddenly he noticed a rope on a pulley at the top of the gate-house. He stood up in the swaying, rattling cart. Then he took aim ... and fired.

The arrow flew through the air and cut the rope – and the gate came crashing down!

The Sheriff was trapped inside his own castle.

A little while later Robin, Marian and Mum stopped deep in the forest.

"Did you see the Sheriff's face?" laughed Robin.

"I did," said Marian. "He'll never forgive us for making him look so stupid."

"That's why we can't go home," said Mum. "I've got a better idea, though. We could live in the forest and fight for fairness."

"Fantastic!" said Robin. "I've always wanted to be an outlaw …"

That's just what they did, of course. Others came to join them in the forest, and soon the Sheriff was very afraid of Robin Hood and his band of outlaws ... and above all, of Robin's mum!